Nine Fruits *of the* Spirit

A Bible Study on Developing Christian Character

Kindness

Robert Strand

New Leaf Press

A Division of New Leaf Publishing Group

First printing: June 1999
Third printing: September 2009

ISBN-13: 978-0-89221-468-6
ISBN-10: 0-89221-468-6
Library of Congress Number: 99-64013

Cover by Janell Robertson

Printed in China

Please visit our website for other great titles:
www.newleafpress.net

For information regarding author interviews, please contact the publicity department at (870) 438-5288.

Contents

Introduction

There is an ancient story out of the Middle East which tells of three merchants crossing the desert. They were traveling at night in the darkness to avoid the heat of the day. As they were crossing over a dry creek bed, a loud attention-demanding voice out of the darkness commanded them to stop. They were then ordered to get down off their camels, stoop down and pick up pebbles from the creek bed, and put them into their pockets.

Immediately after doing as they had been commanded, they were then told to leave that place and continue until dawn before they stopped to set up camp. This mysterious voice told them that in the morning they would be both sad and happy. Understandably shaken, they obeyed the voice and traveled on through the rest of the night without stopping. When morning dawned, these three merchants anxiously looked into their pockets. Instead of finding the pebbles as expected, there were precious jewels! And, they were both happy and sad. Happy that they had picked up some of the pebbles, but sad because they hadn't gathered more when they had the opportunity.

This fable expresses how many of us feel about the treasures of God's Word. There is coming a day when we will be thrilled because we have absorbed as much as we have, but sad because we had not gleaned much more. Jewels are best shown off when held up to a bright light and slowly turned so that each polished facet can catch and reflect the light.

Each of these nine jewels of character will be examined in the light of God's Word and how best to allow them to be developed in the individual life. That is how I feel about the following three verses from Paul's writings which challenge us with what their Christian character or personality should look like. Jesus Christ has boiled down a Christian's responsibility to two succinct commands: Love the Lord your God with all your heart, mind, soul, and body, and love your neighbor like yourself. Likewise, Paul the apostle has captured for us the Christian personality in nine traits:

> But the fruit of the Spirit is love, joy, peace, patience, kindness, goodness, faithfulness, gentleness, and self-control. Against such things there is no law. Those who belong to Christ Jesus have crucified the sinful nature with its passions and desires. Since we live by the Spirit, let us keep in step with the Spirit (Gal. 5:22–25).

At the very beginning of this study, I must point out a subtle, yet obvious, distinction. The "fruit" of the Spirit is a composite description of what the Christian lifestyle and character traits are all about — an unbroken whole. We can't pick only the fruit we like.

Unlocked in these nine portraits are the riches of a Christ-centered personality. The thrill of the search is ahead of us!

Kindness

CHRESTOTES, (Greek) pronounced
khray-stot'-ace, meaning: useful moral
excellence of character or demeanor,
gracious, gentle, goodness, and kindness.

THE FRUIT OF THE
SPIRIT IS . . . KINDNESS

Kindness in our rough and tumble, give-no-quarter, shark-eat-shark kind of world is not very high on the characteristic list of most people. Who wants to be kind when you need to be tough and ruthless?

Theological Insight:

The original Greek word is chrestotes, which can mean: "To be mellowed, to be mellowed with age, a person who doesn't act harshly or inflict pain on others, a person who acts different than the serpent, a person who acts in gentleness, and excellence in spirit."
This word carries a broad application of excellence in conveying gentleness and kindness in all interpersonal relationships. In other words . . . someone you'd love to have for a friend.

Who wants to look out for others when you are busy looking out for #1?

Let's set the record straight at the outset . . . kindness is not weakness or wimpishness! It is not a compromising of the truth. It doesn't give in to evil. Kindness is the way in which you act and speak. It's an attitude, a quality of character that stands firm — yet doesn't have to beat down another in order to stand tall. It has a wide meaning.

Jesus Christ is kindness incarnated! In His life and ministry He embodied kindness, modeled it, and expressed it. Why was His presence so sought after by women, children, and men? People are attracted to kindness personified. Kindness is planted in seed form, imputed, and ingrained in the new nature of a new Christian under the code name of "fruit." It's ours to be developed by the work of the

Spirit . . . it's to be shown in all of our human contacts. The goal is for each of us to be as kind to others as Jesus Christ in His mercy has been kind to us. KINDNESS IS A SIGN OF GREATNESS! It is intended to pervade and touch our entire nature. It is to replace the harsh and hardness. Jesus was a kind person.

Think a moment of how much the world has been changed because of the kindness of Jesus. In His day, there were very few or no institutions of mercy . . . few hospitals, few shelters for homeless, few places for orphans, few places of protection for the poor. Compare our world with His world. His was a very cruel, harsh place in which to live — ours has created lots of safety nets and places where people can be helped. Think . . . wherever Christianity has gone, the followers of Christ have given themselves to performing many of these acts of kindness.

> Have you had a kindness shown?
> Pass it on;
> 'Twas not given for thee alone,
> Pass it on;
> Let it travel down the years,
> Let it wipe another's tears,
> 'Till in Heaven the deed appears . . .
> Pass it on.[1]

THE KINDNESS OF GOD

For our first study on kindness, let's begin at the beginning. Let's look at the kindness of God. It's a major theme of both the Old and New Testaments.

Please read Psalm 103:1–18 and Titus 3:3–8.

List some of the benefits you have already received because of the kindness of God in your life:

_____

_____

_____

_____

According to the Psalmist, what are some of the kind and loving things God has done for us?

_____

_____

_____

_____

Each human being has specific yet general needs common to all of us, centered around physical, emotional, and spiritual needs. Please show how God's provisions meet these needs:

_____

_____

_____

_____

_____

Which one of God's "benefits" have you experienced this past week?

_____

_____

_____

_____

_____

Are God's benefits limited only to the righteous? Explain verses 6 and 7:

_____

_____

_____

What kind of picture of God is presented to you from this psalm?

_____

_____

_____

To what is the kindness of God likened?

_____

_____

_____

Are there any conditions we must meet in order to experience God's kindnesses?

_____

_____

_____

_____

_____

Now turn to our Titus verses. How important is the "kindness" and "love" of God to being "saved"?

_____

_____

_____

_____

_____

_____

What kind of picture of God is portrayed in this portion of the Word?

_____

_____

_____

Why is it so important that these principles (verses 7–8) be passed on to others?

_____

_____

_____

What are the things which are "excellent" and "profitable" for everybody?

_____

_____

_____

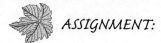

ASSIGNMENT:

• Like David, list the benefits from God which you should be remembering:

_____

_____

_____

_____

_____

_____

• In what ways can you share these truths with someone else?

_____

_____

_____

_____

_____

KINDNESSES WHICH CAN BE SHOWN TO OTHERS

Let me be a little kinder,
Let me be a little blinder
To the faults of those about me;
Let me praise a little more;
Let me be, when I am weary,
Just a little bit more cheery;
Let me serve a little better
Those that I am striving for.

Let me be a little braver
When temptation bids we waver;
Let me strive a little harder
To be all that I should be;
Let me be a little meeker
With the brother that is weaker;
Let me think more of my neighbor
And a little less of me.

(Author is unknown)

Kindness is the harvest of the fruit of the Spirit which primarily benefits others — people with whom we come in contact. And what a crying need there is for people to be kinder. We are experiencing a "kindness-famine." Just stop and think for a moment what kind of an impact a "kinder, gentler" church would have on this world!? How much farther could the gospel be shared when done in kindness? How many people can only be touched through an act of kindness? Think of what would happen inside our churches as people cared in kindness for each other! We have been known as a group which tends to shoot its wounded and hurting. The living out of kindness can change all of that!

Our next study takes us through a number of short verses dealing with

When the kindness and love of God our Savior appeared, he saved us, not because of righteous things we had done, but because of his mercy (Titus 3:4–5).

our subject. Please read Proverbs 14:21, 31; 19:17; Matthew 10:40–42; and Mark 9:33–37.

Do we, as a church, have a problem with the temptation to treat some folk better than we would treat others? If you think so, explain:

_____

_____

_____

_____

_____

Based on the three verses from our Proverbs readings . . . do you think God has a bias toward any specific group of people? If you think so or if you think not . . . please explain:

_____

_____

_____

_____

How does God want us to show kindness to the "poor" and "needy"?

_____

_____

_____

_____

_____

_____

_____

From Matthew 10:40–42, name the specific classes of people mentioned here:

_____

_____

_____

_____

_____

What is our motivation for "receiving" each of these?

_____

_____

_____

What are the specific ways in which we can show kindness to each of these specific classes of people?

_____

_____

_____

_____

Jesus talked about "reward" three times in these verses. What exactly is a "prophet's reward"?

_____

_____

_____

_____

A "righteous man's reward"?

_____

_____

_____

_____

_____

_____

The "reward" for giving a cup of cold water in His name?

_____

_____

_____

_____

_____

Do these promises of rewards motivate you to acts of kindness?

_____

Why or why not?

_____

_____

_____

_____

_____

_____

Now from Mark 9:33–37 . . . what were they arguing about?

_____

_____

_____

_____

_____

Why?

_____

_____

_____

_____

_____

Our world has its concepts of what greatness is all about. How does what Jesus said contradict this?

_____

_____

_____

_____

_____

What was so significant about using a child as an illustration of this truth?

_____

_____

_____

_____

What are some real applications of what it means to "be the very last" and "the servant of all"?

_____

_____

_____

_____

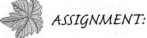 *ASSIGNMENT:*

• It's time for all of us to do a "kindness" checkup. In what specific ways have you been applying the principles of this word when it comes to the poor, needy, children, prophets, disciples, or a righteous person?

_____

_____

_____

_____

_____

• Think of one person whom you know who has been viewed as poor, needy, or lowly by others. In what ways can you give that "cup of cold water" in His name?

_____

_____

_____

_____

_____

> *Jesus called the Twelve and said, "If anyone wants to be first, he must be the very last, and the servant of all"* (Mark 9:35).

THE NECESSITY OF KINDNESS

Kindness is not as highly prized by everyone as it should be. Why? There are lots of people who think that being kind has a too-costly price tag and they are not prepared to pay it. To them, showing kindness can be too time-consuming, too demanding, or too likely to interfere with their own lifestyle, thank you anyhow.

But living the Spirit-filled life is not to be avoided because of any cost, real or imagined. God has set the pace in lavishing His never-ending loving-kindness on each of us on a daily basis through the person of Jesus Christ. In living out the Spirit-filled, fruitful lifestyle it's easy to note that we are to treat others as we have been treated by the Godhead — with sympathy, benevolence, and generosity. All of these character traits and attitudes are practical and usable while being in high demand in all of our relationships. And yes, they are all costly. To be used of God in any genuine act of kindness will involve a cost. The costliest act of kindness was paid when Jesus took upon himself our sins and was nailed to a cross to make atonement.

DO WHAT I CAN

If I can stop one heart from breaking,
I shall not live in vain:
If I can ease one life the aching,
Or cool one pain,
Or help one fainting robin
Unto his nest again,
I shall not live in vain.

(Emily Dickinson)

For our next study, please read what probably is the ultimate biblical portion dealing with our subject of kindness — Galatians 6:1–10.

In your past, do you know anyone who was "caught in sin"?

_____

_____

And how did you treat them?

_____

_____

_____

How do you think your contemporary church members would treat you if you were caught in a gross sin by another member?

_____

_____

_____

_____

If we consider ourselves to be "spiritual," what is the requirement expected of us when another has fallen from grace?

_____

_____

_____

_____

In today's contemporary world, how has this issue and the fallout impacted you and your church?

_____

_____

_____

_____

_____

_____

What do you think Paul means in verse 2 where he tells us to "carry each other's burden"?

_____

_____

_____

_____

_____

_____

How is it possible to make the burden lighter for somebody else?

_____

_____

_____

_____

_____

In what ways are we "fulfilling the law of Christ" by these actions of kindness?

_____

_____

_____

_____

_____

What does Paul have to say to each of us about the process of restoring another?

_____

_____

_____

_____

_____

_____

What are some of the specific pitfalls Paul is warning us about?

_____

_____

_____

_____

_____

_____

How does the law of sowing and reaping relate to being kind to others?

_____

_____

_____

_____

_____

Where do you think the greatest emphasis has been placed here — on restoring another or in checking our own attitudes and actions?

_____

_____

_____

_____

_____

Please explain further:

_____

_____

_____

_____

_____

We have tended to look upon this sowing and reaping in a negative sense only. What did the positive side of this message say to you?

_____

_____

_____

_____

To whom are we to do good?

_____

_____

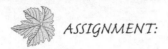 *ASSIGNMENT:*

• In examining all of your relationships and especially those which might need to be restored, give at least one specific example of how you might sow good seed in another person's life:

_____

_____

_____

_____

_____

• In what specific ways can you encourage others in your fellowship to also sow kindness in the living of others?

_____

_____

_____

_____

_____

THE LONG-TERM
BENEFITS OF KINDNESS

There is a wonderful anecdote told about the late President Dwight D. Eisenhower who happened to be vacationing in the Denver area a number of years ago. Somehow his attention was drawn to an open letter to the editor which had a simple request. Six-year-old Paul Haley was dying of incurable cancer and he had wished to see the president of the United States in person.

You can tell a whole lot about a person through their acts of kindness. In this case it was an act which has lived longer than all the presidential speeches he made.

On a Sunday morning in August, the big black presidential limousine pulled to a stop in front of the Haley home, the door was opened by a secret service agent, and out stepped the president. He made his way to the door and knocked.

The door was opened by Donald Haley, barely up for the day, wearing jeans and an old tee shirt and a stubble of a beard. Next to him stood his six-year-old son, Paul. Imagine their amazement at finding the president at their door!

"Paul," said the president to the sick little boy, "I understand you want to see me. Glad to see you." Then he reached out his hand to shake that of the surprised six year old. Then he took him out to see the presidential limo, shook hands with him once more, and left.

Just think of how the Haleys and their neighbors, as well as a whole lot of other American citizens, must have felt when they read the story. Here was one kind, thoughtful deed performed by a very busy president.

Deeds of kindness have a way of living on much beyond the time or effort to do them. They have far-reaching effects and can be wonderfully exciting. Such is the setting of our next biblical text.

Now, let's turn to read our text — Ruth 1 and 2.

What was the problem with Jewish men marrying Moabite women?

_____

_____

_____

_____

Why was it such a difficult thing to be widowed during this time in biblical history?

_____

_____

_____

_____

_____

In Ruth 1:16–17, we have the finest declaration of friendship/relationship to be found in any kind of literature. It's wonderful. What do you think could have caused Ruth to make such a declaration?

_____

_____

_____

_____

_____

Theological Insight:

The name "Ruth" literally means "a female friend." She was a Moabitess, first the wife of Mahlon and then of Boaz, and eventually the ancestress of King David and finally of Jesus Christ. It takes place about 1,100 B.C. in the time of the judges in Israel. Elimelech, an inhabitant of Bethlehem in Judah, emigrated into the land of Moab with his wife Naomi and his two sons. It apparently was a time of hardship which caused this little family to leave their homeland.

In your own words, describe what kind of a homecoming and reaction was accorded Naomi and her Moabitess daughter-in-law:

_____

_____

_____

_____

_____

_____

_____

_____

_____

_____

_____

What kind of a man do you think Boaz was, based on Ruth 2:4–16?

_____

_____

_____

_____

_____

How did Boaz and Ruth meet?

_____

_____

_____

How does kindness on the part of Boaz enter into this story?

_____

_____

_____

_____

How does Ruth react to the kindness of Boaz?

_____

_____

_____

_____

What does it mean to "glean" a field?

_____

_____

_____

_____

And why was she allowed to glean in any field in Israel?

_____

_____

_____

_____

What is the significance of the "kinsman-redeemer"?

_____

_____

_____

_____

_____

The Hebrew term for "kinsman" (*goel*) is used to imply certain obligations arising out of that relationship and has for its primary meaning "coming to the help or rescue of one." The *goel* among the Hebrews was the nearest living male blood relation and on him devolved certain duties to his next of kin. The most striking office of the kinsman was that of the "blood avenger." A wrong done to a single member was a crime against the entire clan. The obligation to avenge fell to the next of kin.

It was also the duty of a kinsman-redeemer to redeem the paternal estate which his nearest relative might have sold through poverty, to act as a go-between in case a person wished to make restitution, and to marry the widow of a deceased relative. This usually fell to a brother (Lev. 25:25, 47; Num. 5:6; Ruth 3 and 4).

How is the long-term multiplying effect of kindness shown in this story?

_____

_____

_____

_____

_____

The most exciting long-term benefit is found in Ruth 4:16–17, 22. Naomi has a grandson and Ruth has given birth to a significant son, Obed, the father of Jesse who was the father of David, whose line brought us Jesus Christ! Write your reaction to this wonderful story with the happy ending:

_____

_____

_____

_____

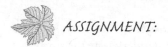 *ASSIGNMENT:*

• Who is one person in your circle of relationships who needs to experience God's kindness as can be shown through you:

_____

_____

• Specifically, what are the steps or actions which you can take in order to show kindness to that particular person?

_____

_____

_____

_____

THE HARVEST OF
KINDNESS FOR OTHERS

Two young men were working their way through Stanford University. Their funds got really low and the idea came to

When you think of doing a kindness, don't put it off. After all, what's the use of doing a kindness if you do it a day too late? There's usually a quick window of opportunity and then it's gone, maybe forever. Timing is everything in being kind to others.

engage the great Paderewski for a piano recital and devote the profits to their room, board, and tuition. The pianist's manager asked for a guarantee of $2,000. The young men staged the concert but when tabulated, the ticket sales totaled only $1,600. The two went to the artist and told him of their efforts. They gave him the entire $1,600 and a promissory note for $400 explaining that they would earn the amount at the earliest possible moment.

"No, boys, that won't do." Then, tearing up the note, he returned the money to the boys and said, "Now take out of the $1,600 all of your expenses and keep 10 percent each for your work, and if there is anything left, give me the rest."

The years rolled by. War came and Paderewski was striving with might and main to feed the thousands in his beloved Poland who were starving. There was only one man in the world who could really help Paderewski. Thousands of tons of food began to come into Poland for distribution. After the starving people were fed, Paderewski traveled to Paris to thank Herbert Hoover for the relief sent to his people. "That's all right, Mr. Paderewski," was Mr. Hoover's reply. "Besides, you don't remember how you helped me once when I was a student at Stanford and I was in a deep hole."

The Bible instructs us to "Cast your bread upon the waters, for after many days you will find it again" (Eccles. 11:1). A kindness given is not a kindness lost — it's an investment that has eternal rewards. Besides, you never know when that kindness given will come back to you.

There's another principle about kindness — do it immediately! When you think of it, don't put it off. After all, what's the use of doing a kindness if you do it a day too late? There's usually a quick window of opportunity and then it's gone, maybe forever. Timing is everything in being kind to others.

For our next look at kindness, let's take a page from the life of David. Please read 2 Samuel 9:1–13.

Can you think of an act of kindness which changed your life?

_____

_____

_____

What were the results?

_____

_____

_____

Why was it so important to David to be able to show kindness to King Saul's family? (For a further look you may want to refer to 1 Sam. 20:12–17).

_____

_____

_____

Saul had done everything in his power to eliminate David. Cite some reasons for David not showing kindness to this family:

_____

_____

_____

_____

_____

What kind of an insight do these acts of kindness tell you about the character of David?

_____

_____

_____

_____

_____

_____

Jonathan was the best friend to David, but he was also the son of Saul. Do you think David was acting only out of fulfilling his vow? Why or why not?

_____

_____

_____

_____

_____

_____

Why was Mephibosheth crippled?

_____

_____

_____

_____

_____

What reasons would Mephibosheth have to be afraid of David?

_____

_____

_____

_____

David didn't only talk about being kind, he took concrete actions. What were the specifics of the actions which David set in motion?

_____

_____

_____

_____

Can you put yourself in the place of Mephibosheth and his little family? How do you think these acts of kindness made him feel?

_____

_____

_____

What kind of an effect do you think this action must have had on the people of Israel?

_____

_____

_____

_____

_____

How many others were blessed because of the kindness shown to one man?

_____

_____

_____

_____

_____

Why was it important that David show kindness?

_____

_____

_____

_____

ASSIGNMENT:

• Write down some of the principles of living and acting with kindness you have learned from this particular study:

_____

_____

_____

_____

_____

_____

• Write down some specific steps you will be taking so that you, too, can be a person of kindness in your relationships:

_____

_____

_____

_____

_____

IN SUMMARY

Kindness is a real harvest of the spirit for others. But it also has a boomerang effect — the more you give it, the more comes back to you. Talk about a sense of well-being with the world. In this case, it truly is much more blessed to give than it is to receive. What a joy!

What is God really like? What is the single quality of character of Jesus Christ that strikes you the most? For me, kindness is very high on that list. One of the most beautiful prophetic verses written about Him is from the pen of Isaiah, "He tends his flock like a shepherd: He gathers the lambs in his arms and carries them close to his heart; he gently leads those that have young" (Isa. 40:11). What a picture of kindness!

Take time to allow gentleness and kindness to grow in your garden of the Spirit. Like any other fruit of the Spirit, this one, too, must grow. You just don't simply decide to be gentle and it happens. This is a work of the Spirit in your life and there are a number of actions which you can do to cultivate gentleness into your character. Let's also consider the opposite.

There is a tragic story about Lenin, revealing much about his inner soul. Vladimir Ulyanov was born in 1870 to a family which would suffer many tragedies in the years to come. Later he used the pen name Lenin to promote his revolutionary ideas. He so wrapped himself in his work that he lost almost all capacity for human

Heartlessness, thoughtlessness, abuse, and cruelty have ruined more than one relationship. Be kind at all times, which may be easier said than done, but oh so needed today.

tenderness. Those close to him knew him to be a most miserable man.

Although married, Lenin gave little love to his wife, Krupskaya. One night she rose exhausted from her vigil beside her dying mother and asked Lenin, who was writing at a nearby table, to awaken her if her mother needed her. Lenin agreed and Krupskaya collapsed into bed. The next morning she awoke to find her mother dead and Lenin still at work. Distraught, she confronted Lenin, who replied, "You told me to wake you if your mother needed you. She died. She didn't need you."

Heartlessness, thoughtlessness, abuse, and cruelty have ruined more than one relationship. Be kind at all times, which may be easier said than done, but oh so needed today.

There is so much hardness in this world that I am convinced that one of the greatest evangelistic movements of our time would come in a renewal of gentleness! People respond to kindness. There still is a need for hellfire preaching and witnessing — but the hungry, the lost, the lonely, the hurting, the heartbroken are seeking for a Savior who is first of all gentle. Gentle leading will help them find the healer of broken hearts.

Too many people are living a lifestyle dominated by fear. They are running through life scared. If they only knew how much they were loved by a gentle God and that His people love and care about what happens to them, it could be life changing!

Be gentle . . . be kind . . . for just about everybody you meet is fighting a battle of some kind. True nobility of Christian character comes from a kind heart!

MAKE ME A BLESSING

Out in the highways and byways of life,
Many are weary and sad;
Carry the sunshine where darkness is rife,
Making the sorrowing glad.

Tell the sweet story of Christ and His love,
Tell of His pow'r to forgive;
Others will trust Him if only you prove
True, ev'ry moment to live.

Give as 'twas given to you in your need,
Love as the Master loved you;
Be to the helpless a helper indeed,
Unto your mission be true.

Make me a blessing,
Make me a blessing,
Out of my life . . . may Jesus shine;
Make me a blessing, O Savior, I pray,
Make me a blessing to someone today.
(Ira B. Wilson)

And the fruit of the Spirit is . . . KINDNESS!!

1   Henry Burton, *Encyclopedia of Religious Quotations* (Grand Rapids, MI: Fleming H. Revell Co., 1965).

Nine Fruits of the Spirit

Study Series includes

Love

Joy

Peace

Patience

Kindness

Goodness

Faithfulness

Gentleness

Self-Control

Robert Strand

Retired from a 40-year ministry career with the Assemblies of God, this "pastor's pastor" is adding to his reputation as a prolific author. The creator of the fabulously successful Moments to Give series (over one million in print), Strand travels extensively, gathering research for his books and mentoring pastors. He and his wife, Donna, live in Springfield, Missouri. They have four children.

Rev. Strand is a graduate of North Central Bible College with a degree in theology.